"Alina Celia Cumpan is a rare poet. Renowned for her literary work in her home country of Romania, she made the difficult transition both to a new county and a new language in 2010. In doing so, she has achieved – what so many of us achieve – the impossible challenge of changing one's life completely. Not only has she had her poetry from Wasted Gift (2015) and Unselfish Selfie (2017) published in English (in translation), she has now written a riveting volume of poetry in her adopted language English. In Immigrant of the Planet Cumpan explores her multiple identities as a philosopher and artist. I highly recommend this book to all readers and especially to philosophers, dreamers, immigrants, poets, the children of immigrants, foreign language learner, conscious and engaged citizens, readers concerned with living a better life, and readers desiring a more just future for humanity and the world."

— **Cristina A. Bejan**
Author of Green Horses on the Walls

"I had never imagined myself as an immigrant. What a narrow view. While I am first generation Italian, I grew up in the United States, am raising my family here and expect, one day, to breathe my last amidst the hardscrabble soil of the Midwest. But I am so much more. Immigrant of the Planet unveils a narrative much deeper than where our feet lay. In the end, Alina Celia Cumpan teaches us we are all connected. We are mothers. We are fathers. We are unabandoned, unapologetic lovers. We are heartbroken soldiers of life. We are workers, working the land of possibility. We are people searching for our purpose in unfamiliar territory every day, all the time, whether we have struck new ground in a new country or never left the town we were born in.

Welcome to the world. Your greatest adventure awaits. Immigrant of the Planet is your passport. Happy travels."

— **Michele Kelly**
Fiction writer and contributing author to Today's Inspired Leader

IMMIGRANT OF THE PLANET

Alina Celia Cumpan

IMMIGRANT OF THE PLANET

© Copyright 2021, Alina Celia Cumpan
All rights reserved.

No portion of this book may be reproduced by mechanical, photographic or electronic process, nor may it be stored in a retrieval system, transmitted in any form or otherwise be copied for public use or private use without written permission of the copyright owner.

Artwork by Jahid Hassan
Book Layout by DG. Marco Álvarez
Printed in the United States of America

ISBN: 978-1-952779-83-1
Library of Congress Number: 2021903718

The truth brings us closer,
and takes us further.

To my good friend **Daniel Onofrei,**
who inspired me towards
a new journey.

Contents:

As if it weren't..........................pg. 13

...it wouldn't be told....................pg. 65

Instead of preface

LIFE is a foreign language.
You don't need to understand,
You need to feel.
Play
With your pains.
Play
With your thoughts,
Play
With yourself.
Playing you LIVE.

The Author

IMMIGRANT OF THE PLANET

Alina Celia Cumpan

As if it weren't

Status

I'm just an immigrant
of the planet
but my spirit
is a citizen
of the Universe.

The Big Road

We arrive leaving,
we leave arriving,
we live
on the border
between
arrival and departure
this journey
called life.
We live!

Fact

It doesn't matter where and when
you were born
it matters when you met yourself.

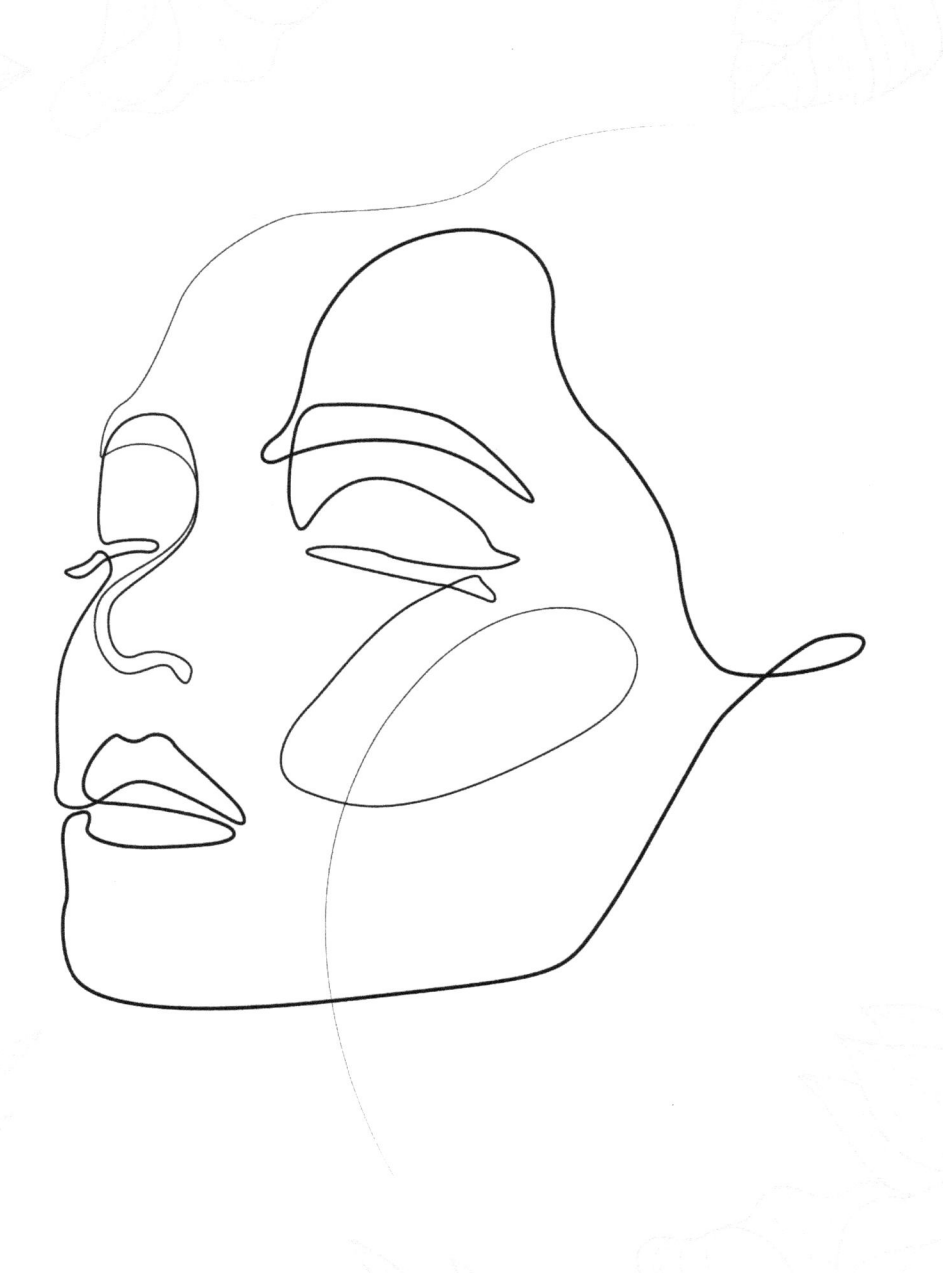

Wish

I would like to understand
more from less
and give everything to the world
from nothing.

Loneliness

In hidden survival talents,
what a poor fortune
what a rich poverty
it's loneliness!

Announcement

Reminder
for those infected
with overthinking virus:
Nothing lasts forever!
Act!

Release

Knock down the prejudice wall
in the name of the freedom -
for the freedom of your mind!

Advice

Stop controlling!
Don't keep anything too tight.
Everyone, everything and
even every thought
needs space to grow.

Skip I

Skip the understanding,
Go straight to the acceptance
someone told me once
without knowing
that his advice
it will become a mantra (for me).

Skip II

**Skip the judgments and
go straight to love;
Skip the "I" and be humble, unselfish**
I advised others
as a reminder for myself.

Ten Commandments

My ten commandments are:
1. Love
2. Love
3. Love
4. Love
5. Love
6. Love
7. Love
8. Love
9. Love
10. Love

This is my Decalogue of life and hope.

Introduction

- Free Spirit, what's your name?
- My first name is **EmbraceTheUnknown,** my middle name is **TrustTheTruth**
and last name is
LoveUnconditionally.

Places of Time

It's a plank of
"once upon a time"
between us
it is called past;
It's the pregnancy test
of the question
between us
it is called future;
It's a drop of
"as much as necessary"
between us
it is called present.

True connection

I have nothing to do with you,
just with your soul!
The rest is freedom.

Statement

I want a one life stand with you;
keep the change!

Half and Whole

Me – a half without a half
You – the other half
Us – repeated searches completed.

Promise

I promise to take care of you
just like I take care of myself.
I promise to love you
Just like I love myself.
I promise to forgive you
like I forgive and can't forgive myself.

My love

I forgive myself
for loving you all
so much.
Now, forgive me
because
I could not love you all
forever.

Get lost

Get lost
in the colorful shadows of autumn
in winter amnesia
in the green of repeated springs
in the rain of summer rainbows.
Get lost...
Get lost to find yourself.

Towards Progress

We live in times of unclear forms
with bizarre speed
in which we are asked to adapt.
Upgrade yourself,
do it constantly
but
without forgetting your roots.

Do it!

Don't wait for anyone
to cover
the hole from your soul.
Fix yourself!

Advice

In the universe
of emotional blackmailers,
help only those who deserve it!

Why?

There is a question with millions of answers.
Why?
Why is the key
to all the comedies and tragedies
in our lives.

Ingratitude

When we don't want to blame ourselves
we blame God
thinking that's why He's There.
Wrong.

The Dilemma of an Immigrant Writer

It's been years
since I don't know
in what language to write
in order to write better.
Should I write in the one I want
or the one I need?
In the language I want,
what I need is missing,
in the language I need
what I want is missing
and yet, I write...

...it wouldn't be told

Work Permit

My dreams
received
the work permit
before me
in America.

True Story

As a new immigrant to this country
I was fired once.
My boss, a psychologist,
she fired me because I was unhappy
doing cleaning in her house.
She knew I could do more,
and I did.
Give credit to those who have survival jobs.
For a loaf of bread some of us
bury talents.

How?

I wonder
how to raise myself
so I can grow
what needs to be grown,
how to see myself
so I can see
what needs to be seen,
how to take care of myself
so I can take care
of what needs taking care,
how to teach myself what needs to be learned,
how to love myself
so I can love
what needs to be loved.
I don't wonder
Why
by loving
I learn
to take care of everything,
watching
what I want
to grow.

Peace in Within

I unfriended my EGO.
Since then, no more glitches
in the matrix.

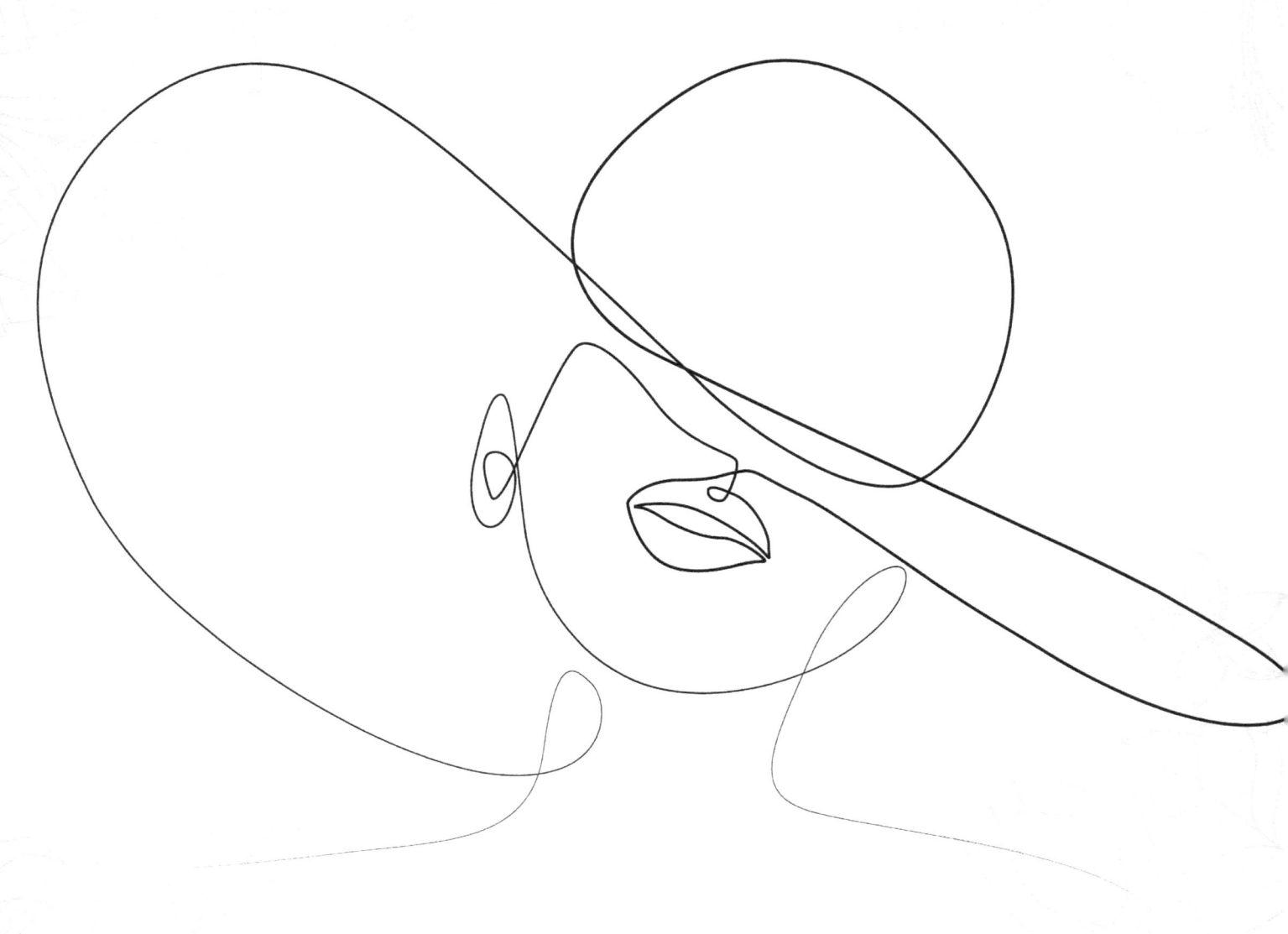

Inside Myself

The mother told me 'be mother'
The father told me 'be father'
The child told me 'be child'
The angel told me 'be an angel'
You told me 'be yourself'
I lived... melting them all inside myself.

Stories

From the acceptance of emotions
were born
the most beautiful stories.

On My Own

My escapes
were the most beautiful
encounters with myself;
In their flight
I gave birth
to feelings,
to ideas
and I was born on my own.

New Hobby

We collect joys and bury traumas,
but let's not forget …
when the joys pass,
we are left with memories only;
when tragedies pass,
we remain with peace, joys and memories.
Let me tell you a secret:
I have a new hobby
I like to dig up my traumas.

True Connection

Some people
stick to your soul
like bark on a tree.
Next to them,
emotions do not die.

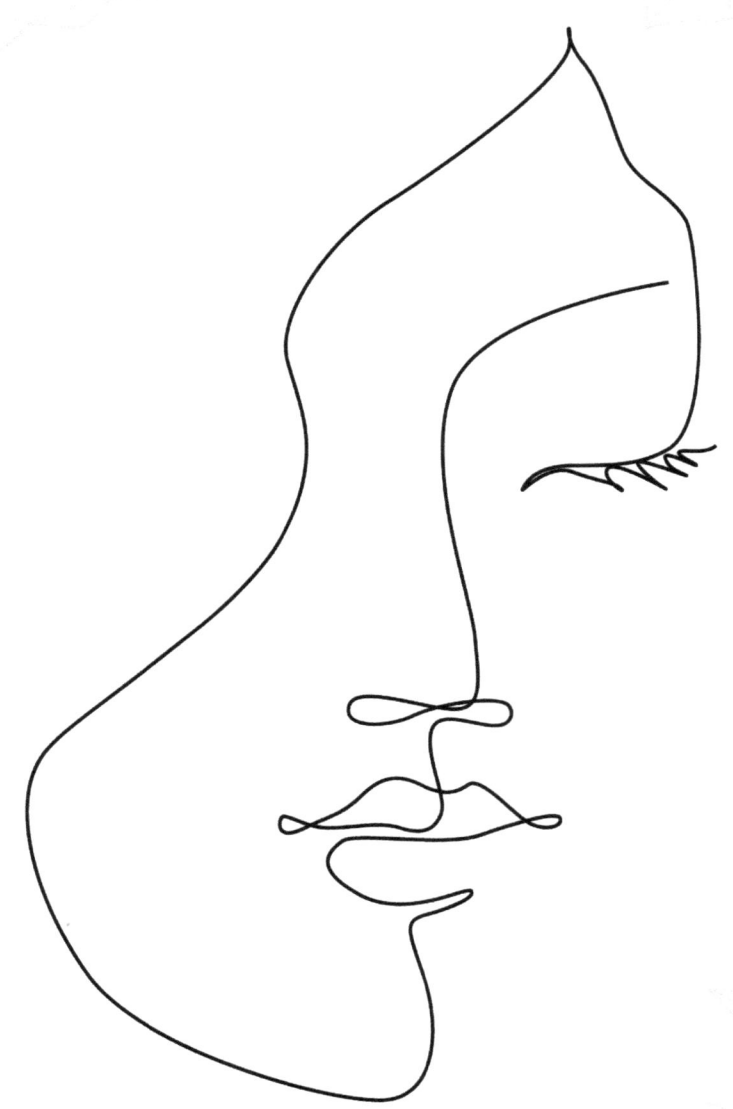

Soul First

How beautiful are the people
untouched by worries,
uncontaminated by shadows,
surrounded by good thoughts
without indications on how to use
the heart.
How beautiful is the human –
that caress the soul...

Dialogue

- Tell me,
  Where is the middle of nowhere?
  Where is the center of everything?
  Over there I'll find you…
- Over there you'll find yourself.

Let me

I feel
that you are going
through some emotional
turbulence,
but let me in.
I can handle
all your scars.
Let me cut
your nails
grown
on the heart.

Immigrant Love I

When I didn't know the language
of the country
I moved to,
I fell in love
with the story of gestures, of looks,
not of the words made into a story.

On My Way

I've been to some storms
where broken hearts go;
On the way back,
trying to gather myself,
I met with some hard-working hands.
Those hands
can bandage
unborn tears
without knowing.

Circle

The one who runs away from you,
runs away from himself.

Immigrant Love II

I can't marry you!
Go back home!
His love flew,
my tears flowed,
but time covered the pain.
Understandable in the end -
He was an immigration officer
I was an immigrant with a case in pending.
His kisses
remained
bruises
not on my lips.
My house was him
but it was only an abandoned house.

Odd number

You don't know,
but I used to see you
as my winning PowerBall
when you made me feel
just an unlucky scratch card for you.
Still, I endorse your karma.

Conclusion

The story between us
if it's true,
it explains a lot,
if it's not,
it explains
everything.

San Pedro

Without asking me for time,
they all wanted my love
and I love them...
for a while.
Then, you came,
gave me time,
and pushed me to love myself.
Since then,
I start to love
without time.

Shadow

Plant carefully
the seeds of your soul
in the souls
of your children.
From your harvest
you will feed on old age.
The future of the world
will be in their hands
so is your world.

Mother Nature

Someone is crying
without tears
in the hospital of the Earth.
Please proceed the checking
with a X-ray of desires.
Mother Nature
needs our love,
not our tears.

Differences

Look into the eyes before looking at the skin color.
Listen to the soul, not to the accent.
Respect, don't judge –
LOVE
everyone is born with a gift,
everyone holds on to a hope.

Never Complain

I could never complain
that it's hard for me
to be a single mother.
Mary raised Jesus alone
in more difficult times.

Signs

I received many signs in life.
I made another galaxy from each point
from commas, waves
hug from parentheses
story, out of the question
cross, from exclamation
birth, in silence.

Life

Somewhere in the world
someone is born
someone is dying
and in the middle
it hurts.

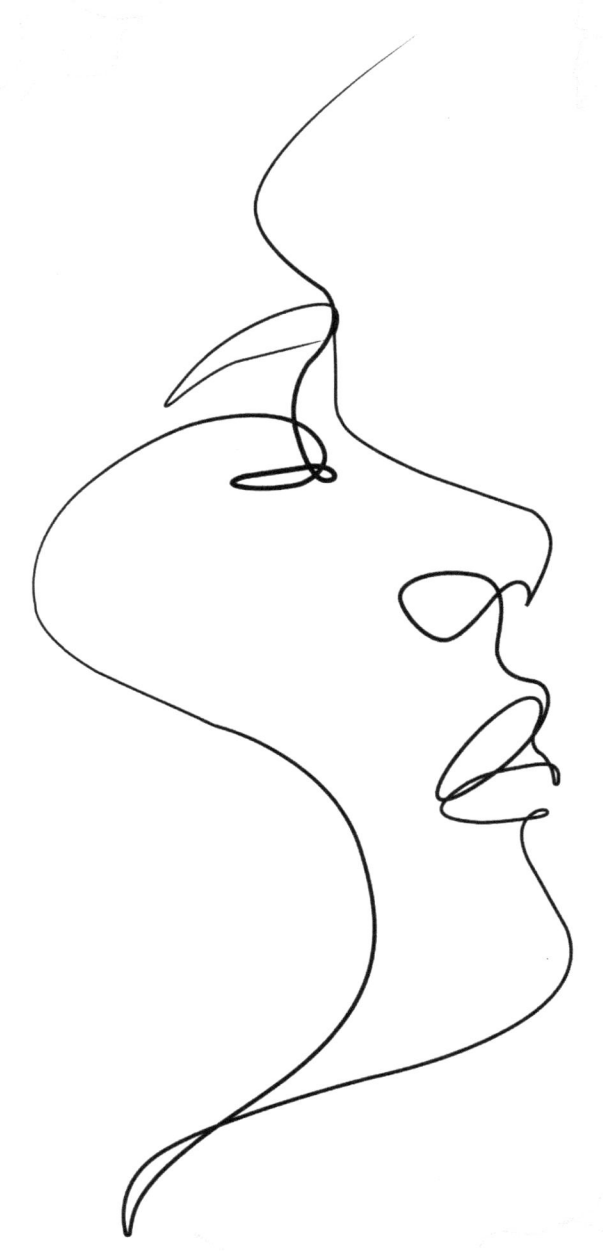

Key

Music has changed
and will change
the face of the soul.
A sound,
a shout
can change the world.
Listen to the birds of the earth
and to troubadours
of the planet -
the tongues of hope are they.

Where Poetry is Born

There are no perfect words for poetry,
just perfect moods for words.
This is how poetry is born.

Instead Of Closing

Look, over there are all the animals of the earth...
the mouse scared of the cat,
fearless vulture and the seagull,
the dolphin and the shark,
brave lion
and the gentle deer,
the snake that frightens,
the watchdog
and the caressing cat.
They are all here...
in me,
in you,
Immigrant to the planet.

About the Author

ALINA CELIA CUMPAN
Poet, editorialist, and cultural activist

Having been raised in Romania, she received a Master Degree in Public Administration Management and two Majors in Political Science and Economical Science along with other educational programs in diplomacy, migration, and youth policies.

Photo by Marian Petruța

She published other 3 poetry books - *Between Two Worlds and Me* in 2007, *Wasted Gift* in 2015, and *Unselfish Selfie* in 2017. She has proven her commitment to public service and cultural projects and has been the president of the Authentic Society for Language and Romanian Culture of Chicago since 2017.

Publisher Note

When we first heard about Alina's concept of the book, we completely fell in love with it. Being an "Immigrant of the Planet" has so many meanings that we can treasure in our hearts. A great book idea always begins with a single connection that leads to a conversation with an author. That initial conversation with Alina sparked pure possibility and opportunities to make an impact and create magic together.

For us, as a multicultural media company that celebrates every milestone of the author, this book has a very special meaning. We have worked with authors with many different types of backgrounds, traditions, and of course stories. Each author brings unique qualities to their author journey and Alina was no different. Alina brought a brightness and purposeful mind to our work together. Her desire to touch readers with her powerful words evoked endless inspiration to our team throughout the process. The poems that Alina crafted were carefully molded into touching messages that are sure to spark ideas and powerful emotions into her readers.

Her book, "Immigrant of the Planet," touches on themes that are truly universal. As human beings we are all united together not only by our physiology but by our hearts and souls. Human connections and self-awareness is key to living a life of significance. Her poems speak so eloquently on what it means to be an immigrant of this world and how culture truly transcends beyond any boarder. It shines light to the ideas that we all have dreams and will fight and travel to the ends to reach them. We are so proud to have been a part of Alina's journey. Thank you Alina, for your trust in us and allowing us to be bring this magical book to life. You are amazing!

With lots of gratitude,
-FIG FACTOR MEDIA

www.ingramcontent.com/pod-product-compliance
Lightning Source LLC
Chambersburg PA
CBHW042357280426
43661CB00096B/1141